Government and the Economy

Enriching Language and Literacy through Content

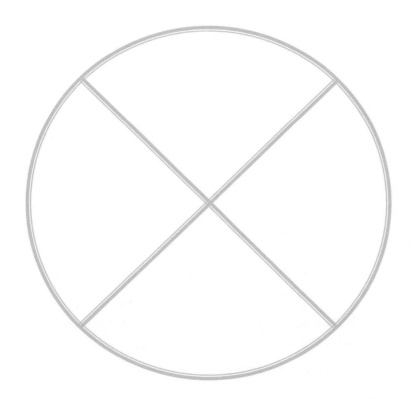

Our Government and Us Series

EDDEIN Literacy Team

To order additional copies of this book, contact:
Xlibris
1-888-795-4274
www.Xlibris.com
Orders@Xlibris.com

Author's Note to Users

This text presents several useful strategies for instructional and learning purposes. The book is structured to:

- Build Learners Conceptual Skills: Every chapter in this text sets of with a conceptual question that drives the instructional and learning processes. This strategy ensures that instructors are guided and can ensure that conversations are pointed, and related to the uncovering of the answer to each question.

- Critical Vocabulary development: Embedded in each chapter and within its conceptual scope is a set of essential vocabulary. The words are contextually used to provide learners an opportunity at weaving out the meaning. Additionally, the text contains a dictionary component that delves deeper into words, their context of usage, usage variety and actual sentence examples for students to replicate. As a precursor to engaging each chapter, pre-teaching the chapter vocabulary is recommended.

- Making the Connections: Teachers are encouraged to ensure that specific point is made to connect concept, vocabulary and their relationship to government and its role in the economy. Additionally, promote civic literacy will require learners to provide verbal and written narratives around key issues and concepts. Teachers are further encouraged to draw on global experience, within and outside of the classroom to reinforce concepts, expand learners' knowledge and understanding.

- Building Academic Skills: Teachers must necessarily utilize text to strengthen learners' capacities to analyze relationships – connectional, causal, comparison, in addition to reading, writing, listening and speaking using the content. Teachers may, additionally, use the text to build students problem-solving skills by developing projects and learning activities that utilize those skills, especially when introducing students to economic policies and its uses.

TABLE OF CONTENTS

1

HOW IS GOVERNMENT INVOLVED IN THE ECONOMY?

To run a country, there is a lot of work that a government must do. One of the many jobs of the government is to manage the economy of a nation. Managing the economy is a job given to the government by the Constitution. The Legislative, Executive and Judicial branches are important in the making, enforcing and interpretation of laws that affect the economy. To manage the economy, the Constitution separates what the federal and state governments can and cannot do.

The Constitution states that jobs not given to the federal government are reserved for the states. There are, however, some things that both the federal government and the States do together. Collecting taxes, buying goods and services, and managing the national economy are some of the jobs carried out by both the federal and state governments.

Another important job of the government is the protection of citizens' economic rights. The Constitution guarantees citizen's rights. It is the responsibility of government to ensure that those rights are always protected.

2

WHAT'S AN ECONOMY AND WHO ARE ITS AGENTS?

An economy is a system of managing how goods and services are produced, distributed and consumed. In the economy, there are many agents. They are grouped as producers and consumers. There is no economy without producers and consumers.

Producers are people who make goods and services for others to buy and use. Producers come in different forms. Farmers, bakers, painters, teachers, doctors are all producers. They make or provide things that people need and use. Anyone can be a producer. Whether it's making breakfast for the family, cleaning the house, baking a cake for a party, people produce every day, production takes place in many ways.

The other group of people in the economy are consumers. They are the people who buy and use goods and services from producers. There are many consumers around us. We are consumers because we use different things every day. When students ride the school bus, eat lunch, listen to a teacher, buy a new backpack, or help a friend eat up a cake, they are consuming. Consumers are important because without consumers, goods and services will not be made or used.

There are lots of goods and services around us. Products are things made that we can see and touch. They are tangible. Examples of goods are pencils, notebooks, fruits, cars, phones, houses, sofa, and clothes and so on. Services, on the other hand, are intangible products, that cannot be touched, but their results can be seen or measured. Doctors, teachers, painters, drivers, chefs, janitors provide services that people benefit us.

The economy is important because through it, people get what they want. Stores and malls are open with lots of goods in them when the economy is in a boom. When the economy is in a recession, prices are high, and it is difficult to find or buy many things.

3

HOW DOES THE GOVERNMENT MANAGE THE ECONOMY?

It is the government's job to make sure that the economy is always good. The government uses taxes collected to support producers provide goods and services for consumers, and to keep the economy working properly.

Furthermore, government manages the economy using policies. Policies are the plans, government hopes, will help the economy function well. Economic policies are a set of plans government uses to ensure that the economy is working well. The government uses fiscal policy, monetary policy or both to manage the economy. When the government gives subsidy to businesses or reduces taxes for people, they are keeping more money in peoples' hands. With more money, people can buy more goods and services. A policy that keeps more money in the hands of people is an example of a fiscal policy.

On the other hand, when the government increases the cost of borrowing money from the bank or reduces the supply of money from the economy, the people have little money to spend. This is an example of a monetary policy. The government uses fiscal, monetary policy or both to manage the economy.

4

HOW DOES GOVERNMENT GET MONEY TO DO ITS WORK?

Tax collection is the most important way government gets money to run the country. Congress makes laws on how much taxes the executive branch can collect from working people, businesses and property owners. The Executive branch, whether at the federal, State or local levels then goes ahead to collect taxes. Taxes are used by the government to provide goods and services for the people. The government pays the military, the police, firefighters, and much more to serve and keep the population safe. Government provide schools, parks, libraries and much more for the good of the people.

The federal government collects taxes from working people and businesses. State governments also collect income taxes and other fees from people in each State. Professionals such as teachers, doctors, lawyers, and businesses pay licensing fees to legally operate in each State.

As people earn income, they buy houses, cars, boats and many other things that cost a lot of money. On such things, people pay property taxes to the county in which they live. For example, the owner of a house in Stafford County, Virginia will pay property tax to the County government every year. People pay high property taxes in counties that are very expensive, and low property tax in counties considered inexpensive.

At the City level, people pay sales taxes on small money items like watches, shoes, clothes, and burgers at McDonald's etc.

5

HOW IS OUR ECONOMY CONNECTED TO ECONOMIES OF OTHER COUNTRIES?

Another important job of the government is to manage trade with other countries. Trade is the exchange of goods and services between producers, and consumers. Regulating trade between our country and other countries is important to protect citizens from poor quality and harmful imports.

Imports provide an important source of supply of goods and services to our economy. Because many people in our country are immigrants from other countries, they desire things from their native countries sometimes. Also, things from other countries are often cheaper than those made in the US. Some imports from other countries include tropical fruits, cars, electronics, clothes, technical skills and so on.

International trade is important because local producers have a chance to export their products to foreign markets as well. Many producers make a lot of money manufacturing products for other economies. Like the United States, exports are an important way other countries make money. The US exports cars, technology, and services to many countries around the world. The United States and China are prosperous countries because they export lots of goods and services to other countries.

Goods from countries with which the US has an excellent relationship may be exempt from paying taxes or tariffs. Usually, this is done to enjoy a similar action from another country. The United States, Canada, and Mexico are part of the North America Free Trade Agreement (NAFTA). NAFTA is an agreement between the countries to promote trade within the region between the three countries. The are many other similar agreements around the world.

Whenever local producers are doing poorly, and not making enough money, the government uses taxes to help them stay in business, keep employees and ensure that the economy doesn't go into recession. The government uses some of the collected taxes to support local businesses during a recession. The government gives out subsidies to companies to keep them from shutting down. During the recession of 2008, President Obama provided subsidies to many American businesses to help keep them working for the people.

6

WHY DOES GOVERNMENT PROTECT OUR ECONOMIC RIGHTS?

In 1792, the Bill of Rights was added to the Constitution. The first ten amendments list the rights every citizen can and must enjoy, and which should be protected by the Constitution. Of their many rights listed in the Amendments, one of the freedoms citizens in the US enjoy is that of the right to make choices. People choose whether or not to join a religion, vote, buy or sell, make friends, speak or go to college. These are examples of the religious, political and economic freedoms that citizens enjoy.

Every government promises to protect the rights of citizens. Protecting citizens' economic rights is important in the economy. When their economic rights are protected, citizens can choose to buy or sell whatever is legally allowed. Whether it is a product or service, citizens have a choice that cannot be taken away from them. In a democracy, protecting citizen's economic rights is a critical job of the government. Protecting citizens' economic rights makes the economy strong. In countries where citizens' economic rights are taken away or limited, the economy is very often not strong.

The right of citizens to own property is an economic right. Property is anything of value that belongs to people. There are different types of property, private and public property. Private and public property. Property owned by a person or group of people are called private property. People are pleased whenever they own a property. Property is a symbol of wealth. Rich people have a lot of private property. Examples of private property includes a person's clothes, houses, boats, bikes and so on.

On the other hand, property owned by the people and managed by the government is public property. Public property is generally used by everyone, regardless of their race, religion, economic status or their political connections. Parks, libraries, public schools, roads, are all examples of public property that is available for use by people in the population.

It is, therefore, important to note that government does not only pay for goods, but also pay teachers, the police, health workers, lawmakers, and thousands more, for the services they provide to keep the government operating. Some payments made by government to service providers are made in the form of salaries to government workers.

The government is therefore essential in how well the economy works. Making sure that citizens elect the best government is as important for the country.

GOVERNMENT & THE ECONOMY

CIVICS DICTIONARY SERIES

BOOM

- **Boom** *(noun) – in economics, a boom is a condition in which the economy is performing well.

Boom (present)
    Ex. Our business is experiencing a boom.

Booming (Present Progressive)
    Ex. The economy is booming.

Boomed (Past Tense) –
    Ex. Last year, my business boomed and I made lots of money.

BUDGET

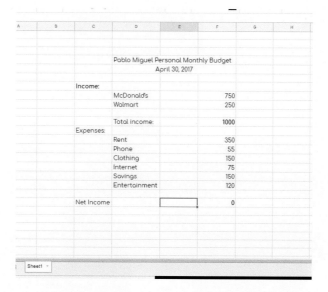

- **Budget** * – a financial plan of how to get and spend money.
- Context - used whenever one expects to receive and spend money.

Budget (Noun) - A financial plan of the government for receiving and spending money
   Ex. The Executive presented the national budget to congress for approval.

Budget (Verb) – The act of creating a budget.
   Ex. My family budgets for every major spending during the year.

   Ex. Karen budgeted to buy her new car.

CONSUMER

- **Consumer** * – all users of goods and services.

Consume (Verb) – To use goods and services.
  Ex. We're hoping to consume a whole pizza.

Consumed (Past tense) -
  Ex. The children consumed all their vegetables.

Consumption - (Noun) – The act or process of consuming.
  Ex. During our consumption of the pizza, Juan choked.

ECONOMY

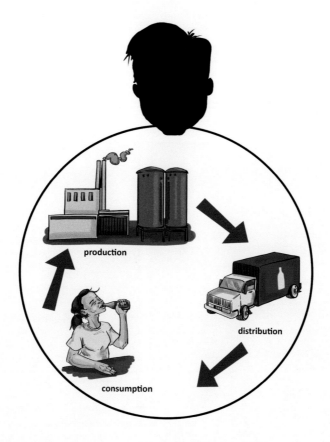

- **Economy** – the system of production, distribution and consumption of goods and services.

Economy (Noun) – The environment where buyers and sellers interact.
    Ex. The economy is doing very well.

Economic (Adjective) - relating to economics.
    Ex. Felix's decision to save money was an economic choice.

Economical (adverb) – relating to economics.
    Ex. My dad was very economical with the money he had.

EXEMPT

- **Exempt** *(Verb) – being free from any payment or obligation.

Exemption (Noun) – the state being free from something.
    Ex. We enjoy our exemption from the test.

Exempted (Past) -
    Ex. At the airport, pilots are exempted from standing in lines.

EXPORTS

- **Exports** – products sold to other countries.

Export (Verb) – the act of sending goods and services to other countries.
  Ex. Derrick exports mangoes to Canada.

Exporters (Noun) – people who carry out exports.
  Ex. My father is an exporter of apples to Brazil.

Exportation (Noun) the process of sending goods to another country for sale.
  Ex. I learned a lot about the exportation process from my father.

FISCAL POLICY

- **Fiscal policy** – Government's use of spending and taxation to manage the economy.
- Context: used to describe any action of government that involves the use of taxes and spending.

Fiscal Policy –

    Ex. The government uses fiscal policy to manage the economy.

    Ex. The new governments fiscal policy is to reduce taxes on middle level incomes.

    Ex. The government hopes to increase spending to create more jobs.

IMPORTS

- **Imports** – goods and services brought into a country for sale.
- Context: Used whenever something is being brought in from another place.

Imports (Noun) – things brought in for sale from other countries.
Ex. Did the imports come in on time ?

Import(Verb) - the act of bring in things from other countries for sale.
Ex. We will have to import Mexican mangoes for the party.

Importers (Noun) – people who import goods and services from other countries.
Ex. There are many importers of foreign goods in the United States.

Importation (Noun) – The bringing in of something from a different place for sale.
Ex. Developing countries rely on the importation of goods from other countries.

INCOME TAX

- **Income Tax** – taxes paid to government from income earned.
- Context: used whenever a part of one's income is deducted to pay government.

Income Tax (Noun) -

Ex. I pay my income tax every month.

Ex. My office pays my income tax automatically.

Ex. Government uses income tax to carry out its work.

MONETARY POLICY

- **Monetary Policy** – government's use of money supply and interest rates to manage the economy.
- Context: Used whenever government uses money supply and interest rates to manage the economy.

Monetary Policy (Noun)

Ex. The government uses monetary policy to encourage people to save.

Ex. The Federal Reserve increased interest rates, making it expensive for people to borrow from Banks.

POLICY

- **Policy** – A plan by government of how they want the country to work.
- Context: used whenever government, businesses or people desire things to run in a certain way.

Policy (Noun)

Ex. Being on time to school is a policy of our school.

My parents' policy require that I come home before 10PM on weekends.

PRIVATE PROPERTY

- **Private Property** – things of value owned by an individual or group of individuals.
- Context: Used to show people's ownership of anything.

Private property (Noun) –

Ex. People need permission to enter a private property.

Ex. Our family house is private property.

Ex. The metro and recreational parks are not private property.

PRODUCERS

- **Producer** – individuals or businesses that create goods and services
- Context: used for anyone or organization that creates goods and services.

Producer (Noun) –

    Ex. Our company is a producer of burgers.

Product (Noun) – the result of production which can be touched.

Production (Noun) – the process of producing goods and services.

    Ex. The production process for making burger was smooth.

Produce (Noun) – goods such as those grown on farms.

    Ex. The produce of corn, wheat, and apples were a lot this year.

Produce (verb) – the act of making anything for consumption.

    Ex. We produced a wonderful painting in class today.

PROPERTY

- **Property (Noun)** – anything of value owned by a person, groups of people or a business.
- Context: used when connecting an item to a person or group of people.

Property (Noun) – things of value belonging to people or businesses.

Ex. Our family property in Virginia is a lot.

Ex. The red backpack in the cafeteria is my property.

PUBLIC PROPERTY

- **Public property** – property belong to the public and managed by the government.
- Context: Use for property that anyone can use.

Public Property (Noun)

    Ex. The play ground in our neighborhood is public property.

    Ex. The restaurant serves everyone, but it is not a public property.

    Ex. The National Memorial is a public property.

RECESSION

- **Recession** – A downturn in economic activities when money has very little value.
- Context: used when people need more money to buy fewer things or when jobs are difficult to find.

Recession (Noun) - the condition of lowering economic activities.

Ex. President Obama led the economy out of the recession.

Ex. During the recession, many people lost their jobs.

SALES TAXES

- **Sale tax** – the extra money paid when buying something.
- Context: used when purchasing small money items.

Sales Tax (Noun) -

    Ex. We pay sales taxes on everything we buy.

    Ex. The City government hopes to raise sales tax to support public schools.

SUBSIDY

- **Subsidy** – money given to businesses by government to help keep them working.

Context: Used whenever a business or a lower authority receives help from the government or a higher authority.

Subsidy (Noun) -

Ex. Our school receives subsidy from the State.

Subsidize (Verb) – the action of giving financial help to struggling companies or businesses, especially during a recession.

Ex. General Motor Corporation was subsidized by the government during the recession.

Ex. The price of gas was rising so the government had to subsidize gas companies.

TARIFFS

- **Tariffs** – fees paid for the importation of goods from other countries.
- Context: Used when required to pay a fee for something.

Tariffs – (Noun)

    Ex. The company paid the tariffs on the goods at the port.

    Ex. Increasing the tariffs on imported goods will increase their prices.

    Ex. Goods from some countries pay no import tariffs.

TAX

- **Tax** – Money people pay to government from money earned, things owned and bought.
- Context: Used when making payments to government.

Tax (Noun)

 Ex. Every good citizen must pay taxes and on time.

Tax (verb) – Requiring someone or a business to pay a tax.

 Ex. Were you taxed the full amount ?

Taxation (Noun) – the act of requiring or imposing tax payment on a person or business.

TRADE

- **Trade** – the exchange of goods and services.
- Context: Used when something is exchanged for another.

Trade (Verb) – The act of exchange.
　　Ex. The Cavs traded Kyrie to the Celtics.

Trader (Noun) – A person whose main job is trading.
　　Ex. Emelia is the fruit trader down the street.

Printed in the United States
By Bookmasters